AF412204

*The
Triumph
of Life*

Also by Jean Day

Linear C
Flat Birds
The I and the You
The Literal World
Enthusiasm: Odes & Otium
Daydream

Some of these poems first appeared in *The Delineator*, edited by
Larry Fagin; *Across the Margin*, edited by Richard Roundy;
and *Open House*, edited by Housten Donham and Cosmo Spinosa.
Warm thanks to the editors.

ISBN 978-0-9998350-0-5

Design by Aesthetic Movement.
Printed in the USA.

Published by Insurance Editions
33–28 81st Street, Apt. 31
Jackson Heights, NY 11372

www.insuranceeditions.com

# THE TRIUMPH OF LIFE

JEAN DAY

INSURANCE EDITIONS

# TABLE OF CONTENTS

## *Dixit*



## *Formal Feeling*

## No Dice

*To my siblings*

*Dixit*

# THE CARDINAL'S BALD

Turtleneck: dead.

Summer rain: gone to town.

Morning: no solution.


Some of us want to change the world
Others just to live it
                    (down)


When it's time to go
Come back and tell us

We can see through the act
But we're not magicians


Like,
        goodbye if I don't see you.

## CALL ME OLD FASHIONED

(But call me)
when the pancakes are ready
at mom's house.

What are we going to do with you?

Let the drenching
begin again
Let Castor beat Pollux
to the Punch

      and Judy side
of things; we'll go

when the car
      gets back

from the beach.

## BACK TO THE FUTURE

Oh that old thing?

The chickadee's see
saws the nest

> One's riddle's
> another's struggle

Strength, will—whatever—
remains solvent

> We'll be there
> in our rags

when science comes
> to tap us
for a bone density

test

## YOU KIDS


The ceasefire's falling apart
Where grass grows naked
                    underfoot.


Maybe it's time
to get up and take a tip
from your doctor about that
                    overactive bladder.


Chores, showers.


Entrails wash up
near a recent catch
                    without release.


We tried to protect

        you kids.

TIME WAS


A great George Burns convention.

Don't even ask.

If the question's always
what comes *after*
we'll never get
          anywhere (*on*).

Parents
returning from viewing the news

                    Shake

from the tree that has been
          since before I was born

                    an acorn.

It couldn't get any worse.

ORNERARY

14

"Shit-town"
is our new name
for fathomless.

You'd think us dying
to go ballistic
over here, over where we fear
to tread

       Instead

I made the "L"
in Hell on Wheels
for you to
    ride

like man's incontinence

# VIEW FROM THE LIVING ROOM COUCH

*15*

Birds can't be made
to sing
though a few
have excellent voices

plumage notwithstanding.

The persistence of rain ...

(We're not from here
          or not for generations)

                    ... declines to stir

Nonetheless sand
implied
          (across the pond, out of sight)

brings up something new
every day

NORTH LIGHT

Yet here we are again on foot

weirdly proud of our relation.

Late light on stone face

bakes in white excreta.

New gulls fuss

in sea upon sea

of down.


Across the sound,
          Point Judith.

And between every wave

                a hiccup.


Sandals in hand
when the phone rang

## SUBTERRANEAN AND AS IF

Who, now, will imitate
Elmer Fudd??


I've been away in the woods awhile
yet my view remains
                    uncorrupted.


        In Gaza
the lid's completely off
and our friends are in bad shape.

We can neither sleep nor think nor work
in these conditions.


No joke.


*Be vewy, vewy quiet.*

# I'M JUST A LITTLE GUY

No more, please.


That the goods of weight
                    trouble
          in a little breeze
                means

pixels off the Lake of Great
                (would be green)

if the angle of sex on leave obtained

the resurrection of my gaze.


Avoirdupois may be a sign
of sticking in the game. Still

in the vast eternal plan

engineering's no excuse.

DOUGHNUTS

19

Fly,
like everything else
when a guy

can't keep his shirt on.

Glitter off the pond
          (The job is plodding)

consoles our effervescence
          (The job is building

an island of destroyers for us)

          off the Burma Road
          which used to be controlled but

          isn't now

## NO DAY IS TOO SHORT



To be a little repulsive.

        You can say that again
and still be sawed
in half

        for the days on end
it used to take
to get from here to California.

The impression of life
strains uncontained
                from tell-tales; kids

more or less accidental

when the sun knuckles under

LEFTOVERS



Pull everything out—
even that old wilted salad.

For us the repetition ...

It doesn't matter how many times
we survey the harbor

It's still deep as the corn
        in regiment

# FROM CREPIDULA

22

to the clap
isn't so far

from the way things work
and you
          think

"anthropocene"

coming in yourself like a figurehead
on the ferry.

At bottom
sit the female PhDs

                  just poised

to change your mind
into something plastic

## THERE YOU GO AGAIN

23

How much longer can we keep up
the fiction
that we're waiting
on you?

                  Whose
division of cells
into red states and blue
plums goes
        right on ahead
of the great paradigm
                      shift?

You're "it."

Not that we resist.

DEAD INDIAN

24

I've seen a lot of movies in which
a tough turkey
gets grilled
          on the spot

in the workbook
where pilgrims set up shop.

Those were happy fantasies.

Like drilling the eyes
          out of Rushmore

## IN DECIDUOUS LEAF

                    25


                Just one question

before I leave
my leaning toward the sun
all Leon
            Leonwood Bean cotton canvas canopy
                    covering an absurdly formal

                    navel.

Doesn't the skirt (of the tree)
                        too
have a place under which we decide

how to characterize the project

as grisly, genetic,
                or real?


Wiping out the magic of the mood?

'GLASS

The boredom of the horizon
lurches up on a swell

no Saltine can keep down.


Those were the days.


Eyes peeled for the whistle
at the end
              of Pollock Rip.

              'Glass

made us itch

regardless

HOLD YOUR COURSE


      When the subject slips
Man wants a nap.

      A little this way, that camber

      Farther and farther off
But still so close
         To shore I think you're going to yell
         Bloody murder


      *But it sufficeth not.*



Then Scotch Tape is proposed (for the job)
Known as it is to be wily.

## THE PUPPET IS DEAD

28

Per Monsieur Teste

Pinocchio turns smooth

just when dawn
            wakes to oppose
            its own fine chatter.


It wouldn't be like you
not to lift a finger

            or slumber through the credits.

But somebody smoked these butts
and it wasn't the puppet.

THE REACHES


Face it.
The frost is on the squash
the cow in the corn.


What you do with your life

is your own business (and frankly carnal).


The Art Ass (a private joke)

sits tight on a doughnut the size of
                          tomorrow

as the nose knows to rest
before its big push.


Meanwhile, a great scheme casts off
          (the very masts are pointed blue!)

          with all your siblings in tow

                    delinquent, fast

                    in the flicker of Elmo.

# FROM A DISTANT STAR

Sectarian quiet is a myth.


I knew it would be like this:


Milky sky of late

wild turkeys in traffic

an earlier and earlier dinner.


It pays to be smart
                in any universe.


But we are down to the final call

                for volunteers

*Formal Feeling*

MUSCLE MEMORY
*Where is my guide?*

It's true.
No one asks
for what they don't yet want.


It's the flathead screwdriver
that's never around
                    when you need one,
                          stupid.


The executioner
          has her own needs.
                    *(OK.)*

But this is not just "display."


Hang around
          if you don't believe me.

IF NIGHT GETS ANY OLDER

36

Marry me
but don't keep me waiting

I've got a lot of work to do
        to be a lesson to unload

            on the membership.

    I am

No rest for the lamb
            I have adopted
to undersign the sun
            of newness

Dear one, the left arm aims the

            right fires

at the masterpiece we've made

            of the errand.

## BY DINT


Because of

his fervent valley

I was scarred for life.


The little craft
plied waves of grass regardless
of its dimpled surface.


                And you think
you can bring that dead deer in here
          to exaggerate the mood


          even further??


And *now* I hunt the echo.

# NEITHER IN (THE WORLD) NOR OUT

After the fact
but before the chores
            of the clown chorus

A drink of water tempts fate

conditions thought

in terms proper to music

(the slap in the face you probably asked for)

        going down like a shot

But I have chosen seven straight nights
        of unexpected drink
        at the sink of raging snowmelt
                        *not*

        her intelligent human sister

NOMINATION

Don't ask.

When the time comes.

You aren't listening.

I'm serious, not *dead*.

>If someone (something)
>this or that
>"causes," "leads to," "gives," or "takes"

>a inch

or foundling in a basket:

We call her Exactly
We call her Efficient
We call her In
And call Her

>*That Is.*

FOOT SOLDIER


The winter closures were hard
          on caregivers and workaholics
who saw themselves alike hard

               as cards tipped
          (like Fabriano out of Ingres)

with mud from the bottom of
                the Bay.

. . .

Look out birds!

Here comes the splat dark
season I am
          a maniac mom
          in minus mode

never too old to schlep your shit
never too cold

          for a noogie.

## IN THE EVENT OF CAPSIZE

41

Jacob came to look at my fan.

Turtle soup was on his mind.

But his eyes did not align.


On this fact
I can only ponder
          (hope he can fix the fan).


In the bayou nets caught
on what they thought a stump.


"Even bologna loaf can go in a gumbo,"
      Jabob opines.

        But no stump.

PLINTH

42

No going back now.

No "righting" any reason
though I stand exposed
                if not corrected.


As if itself beheld
the organ of sight's
                sewn shut by you

        whose stitches are too "true"
                to count.


Could not speech
be the free of seem then

        without such evidence?


Bad night?
No doubt.

Holding all the balls afloat
        is harder than it looks
        without fingers to apply.


But who asked you?

WHEREWITHAL


The time it takes to populate
        the shatter zone
                is underfunded

Yet you are welcome on my land

        Pen easy
in the hand of cursive and

        Native to the heart
                attack

Having learned nothing quite yet
but stranded still
        on a wave of laziness.

        *Every last one of us.*


Which is to say

pancakes on Saturday only fortify the TIA

        or occupation of Sunday

        by all who belong there.

## I WAS BORN BORED


Said Flaubert
but that was material
        for another novel.


        Me,
I had a perverse fondness
            for flatness

pretty sure
my time had come and gone

        I signed on
        the next departing steamer

following the mnemos of knots
and stuck
        in a corner compartment.


Much was said
from the top bunk.

MANNERISM

What if distemper's nuts
        are already cracked?

        Destination—played?

If your head's so far up your ass
you can't see Kansas
                Well

The logic of dreams never
                    added up

to intel internal
        to where I stand

        faux in taxidermy, real in Missouri
        glum in pants
                and patent leather boots


*Where'd you say the exit was*
                    *to wit?*

IN FERGUSON


46

Dead center.

The raw young men

               without within (and therefore
     because and after)

must learn to live
in their brothers' trues

mothers' swifter keepers.


The ubiquitous stick swings both ways:

to the orange of the vegetable
or so much to the grave.


Black Friday's a feature of class.


The mistake is thinking myself not part of the picture.

WENT DOWN TO THE CROSSROAD

We are each other's intelligence

but nobody knows me around here

by my allegations

      now so low to the line
      only bugged-out eyes
            divine

        a lay of land in status
          quo

A maw's a maw for awe
          (so)

weaned away
    from complete disclosure:
    nobody here and nothing to eat
        anywhere.


What right (do you think) sticks to a stick

    waved in the air?

BEING


One,

in a long history of
ramps on and off

        Departs in a canoe ...

So the marchers ...

        Go we on in coils
        as brooms and bones bend

before thought turns us back on *Being One*
                        helping not

even the tooth of her
who said she wouldn't snore
                        (of course)

or come again as a racehorse

name of *Wretched*

# RODE HARD; PUT UP WET

49

Get out of the pan
if you don't like the heat.

Helicopters out tonight
     stir up the stars
         and watch
the red and black
    go bareback at

        Who

are riders
and what snake's not
      all tail?

Call me disenfranchised.


*These poems just write themselves.*

THE "IF" CLAUSE


Where we must part
if worlds
         *— O, whither? —*
             Away.

But stay, if what you say is true
             research! Then
      there we go again
unstopped if you are
      who you say
      and not a phantom

        If I am
all things
      being equal and only if
      we understand ourselves to be
           pointing

      to a legitimate watering hole in the wilderness

The money on the walls
            at Cabbage Key
asked only to be left
            in memento mori


Would we hide out there to wait
as the burrow awaits the shell

            (*Dear December* and *Dear All*)
            or a son leaves home to be leaving?

If the amber in the ale's just syrup

Let the leather of your hand salute
                    instead of speaking

SUN GOES, TOO

                              52


And too young
        to be sorry
        for so much Whitman.

Morning pleasant forest fragrant:
It was theirs to begin with
                              all along

I meant the *infundibuliform*

of the mind brisk and cool

with a whisk and tool

                    What then?


As though we feared the facing page turned
neither toward nor against us

UNSAME



At any speed.

Novelty comes along
        by way of alienation

as a welfare case, Say
your termination
        goes a little off the rails

When a toilet overflows
        in a messy dream
        there's hell to pay

quickly fades away

                to know

Cock Robin's nest's
        an island in the Eel

        fruitless

## COME BACK TO BED



As fact.

Then bring your walker closer
and tell me your pretty name.

I don't know why
the "pure products of America"
should go crazy
                    but they do

                    (a)live as wire
in a backwater to which
          there's no boardwalk access

or country gentleman
          to fill his suit to swing:

*It's crying time again; I can see that*
                              *faraway look*
              *in your eyes*

THIS IS THE HOUR OF LEAD

55

Correcting for salt
     *like leaves in a forest all dissimilar*

Correcting for sugar
     *or the sunlit limits of the night.*


Now, about that drink with Caesar:

Why *not* toast sunny austerity?
Why not praise the bitter meal
before we get down
              to eat?


It would be easier to pretend
     we never go there
     (to the tablets *or* the polls)

being ever dishabille
     all over the map.

But this would leave us still farther behind

and deeper
     I say deeper tangled up in shade

*No Dice*

## THEY LOCK THE DOOR WHEN THEY SEE US COMING

59

Theirs is the generation
of no hope whatsoever.


What I know is what I know—nothing special.


Take one waffle
put it on top of another
and watch the butter
                        feel.


What we mean is reproducing
                all over.


I take the egg gingerly and enter.

## CELLBLOCK A


Not what you expected
but good enough to rise

    to the occasion

    (bowl or basin)

        or anal sun (as they used to say)
        though that was one
            for the books then held

        in the library of

where I hatch my escape.


The dummy is fled

without fooling anybody

NIGHT TRAIN


Sad hair, soap.

Loaded.

Rocked gently.


Nobody has good thoughts
in the middle of the night.


Why then should we be limited to experience?


If the soundtrack simulates
              a real night ride

Father! Mother! —

        nowhere to be seen

# AGAINST WHICH NO COLLAR WOULD BE TURNED

62

So as to be amazing
rather than irrelevant

      The wren

knows to fold in
before we're poor again

      in our desert blindspot.

So we're not birds.
Need rain.

      Cannot quit.
      While we're ahead.

CATCHMENT


Since we're not birds
                (not sudden)
and all our lands are private

We have to plan ahead
like turtles in sand

        waiting for an apology.

One pond for rain
One for retention

        Two brains cleave
to the curve around which

                we're pretty sure

she'll be combing

WITHOUT ROUSSEAU

64

Her hair—we are

unromantic (not sodden)
upon a rock

        nor will we
subside
        in the other room
        (figures of doom)

if the present is our blindspot.

        Booty's what
the occupiers keep.


We hold on to everything.

ELGIN MOVEMENT

65

Springs eternal from her head
        an image of perfection

                still to come

Yet the wooden horse
                is all about
not being nailed

souvenirless

        to her toes,

                those
on which had lain our oysters.


*Who, then, are the enchanted people who can afford to live here?*

## BITE THE BULLET

In the sexual sunrise
of the enchanted nap
our lands were continual
              and continuous ...


Do me the honor of a quick escape

Do not "pretend" to be an animal
              finger curled
                        above your head

You know you are.

Now alone on earth.

67

is a pity fuck.
I could use one too.

Let's take a break here
        and review:

The sun is in the sky
        (oh, sorry,
                its reflection).

Moon, in another frame
                did and died
not to spoil the party.


The car is fled.

OVER PICKLEWEED MARSH


68


And we are left
            unhandled.

One's life either is or isn't critique underfoot

            some squidge

on a continuum
        whose arms redden and break off

            when done. *Done*.


. . .


We exclude, yet accumulate
(the poem pretends)

I can't get any more idiosyncratic
and I can't get any less

                    ash
to soap and glass


        Spring breeze
        *knocks us off our guard.*

WARDEN, WARDEN

Listen to me.
Have I not settled your great questions?

. . .


            Got work?
A cow to drain
                  into how your day chews up
                        the register?

Of all the places I've lived
(some of them pretty charming)

what's passed
        stuck not
to any emulsion.


There was always the hole.

BLUEBIRD

70

Qck,
look out
      for the _____ brown fox
      whose shade's *avante la lettre*

      With us he or she
      should technically be

         blue

not a fiction
of good intention


The little dinosaurs sit with us.

      Hard.
      Postmodern.

WHOSE INVISIBLE RAIN

71

(Her wings also missing)
Leaves us gasping

in our attempt to be happy

Must I hold my horse?
Against the upbraiding wind?

It's nuts to ask
to go to Mars

as if you already knew the moral of the story.

But why not give it a try?

## DO NOT FORSAKE ME

72

As if the irreversible
hadn't already occurred.

Yet we set out hopeful
                (without resale)
in close converse
          (in teacups sucked
                    quick to falls)


Those were the days.


*Obviously.*

If this you see.

Shut it down.

OH MY DARLING


Our ships are captured.
                         Write me
the blow-by-blow.

              Allegory's OK
just don't make me
                fuck the captain.

It's time
to unapologize
          for crushing Thumbelina's thimble.

Go ahead, blow the whistle.


Spring is here.

## AND PETE

Whose lung is leaf
              poised
around a title.

        Were we to organize
the forest
        we couldn't in fact inhabit
        the unbearable

        division of labor.

I'll take the colorful language
You, the foundling kids.


              Never mind
              my shattered lips

CHANTILLY LACE



Never second guess
    the guards at the casino.

Foot on throat
    they just want to make you happy.

Never mind
    *It's not a race*
    presupposes
        goodwill of species

        a nibble in a net
                not

*We're in mourning and hot*

## WE CAN'T AFFORD TO LIVE HERE

76

Think of us as a bunch of skeletons
            throwing back shots
                    bathing in dirt

            and liking it.

I don't call that uninspired

because just as often
                    the voice says
our glee is insincere or

*I can't hear*

the drums of the dreadful decades

            near enough to stick it out

MAY DAY


Just because
you bear the tail
of the lower orders
doesn't mean
you can't be trusted.

When we were Europeans
we got paid in kind;

we threw our caps in the air

      After Nature But

I always happened to be at home
when the plant blew

# NIGHT OF THE LIVING DEAD

When we were Epicureans

we nailed up doors with kitchen matches

against slow invader species


(having taught English all our lives
         only partly with our hands)

         gripping the eyes as images


                  slipped of skin`


An actor's genius then:

         a hole was to dig (out of)

         gamely hanging on
         to skinless, boneless
                  chicken

## "THE BITCH IN THE STORM"

79

Matter of factly takes my hat
                upon arrival
rows out beyond the chop
                leaving me far behind.

Beefy, and not at all well dressed.

The lighthouse (*her* house)
                irritates everybody
        and the grudging clouds tease out

                dry rain.

                (a "veritable downpour")


Happy us who lick the salt

off her foul-weather jacket pocket.

# UNFORGETTABLE


That's what you are

To tribal elders vast

In coupons cashed

As writing on the wall of clouds

Attests

Pulling us against her last
                              leg of rhythm

Remembered as material

Having said all along:


*I wish I had some dirt to eat right now*

This edition of The Triumph of Life
is limited to 500 copies, 50 of which
are numbered and signed by the author.

Jean Day has published six books of poetry and several chapbooks, among them *Daydream* (Litmus Press 2017) *Early Bird* (O'Clock, 2014) and *Enthusiasm* (Adventures in Poetry, 2006). Her work has also appeared in numerous anthologies, including *Nineteen Lines: A Drawing Center Writing Anthology* (Roof, 2007), *Best American Poems 2004* (Scribner, 2004), *Moving Borders: Three Decades of Innovative Writing by Women* (Talisman House, 1998), and *In the American Tree* (National Poetry Foundation, 1986, reprinted 2002). She lives in Berkeley, where she works as managing editor of *Representations*, an interdisciplinary humanities journal published by the University of California Press.